DISCOVER
HAWAII
The Big Island

Text by
STU DAWRS

Photography by
PHILIP ROSENBERG

Title page: *Mauna Kea framed by palms, Mauna Kea Beach Hotel. Inset: 'Ōhi'a lehua. This page, clockwise from top left: Young, modern hula performer. Locally handmade water gourds, drum, hula implements. Kona sunset. Bull rider, Parker Ranch rodeo. Molten lava. Local lady enjoys Hāpuna Beach Park. Yellow ginger. Hawaiian god images carved from local wood (ki'i). Opposite, clockwise from top left: Hilo's Kamehameha statue with leis. Very Large Baseline Array radio telescope, Mauna Kea. 'Ōhi'a lehua. Young girl performing Tahitian style dance. Green and white anthurium. Native Hawaiian cultural ceremony, Halema'uma'u Crater. Cruise ship Independence. Boogie boarder in surf. Lava flow to the Pacific, Volcanoes park.*

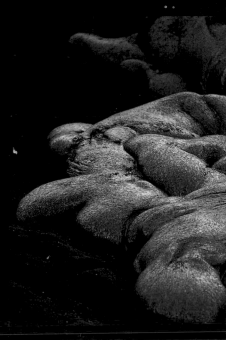

CONTENTS

E KOMO MAI

WELCOME!

IT'S SAID THAT THE REASON half of the island of Hawai'i is lush while the other half is arid has to do with an encounter between the volcano goddess Pele and Kamapua'a—a shape-shifting demigod who most often manifests himself as a boar (that is, a *pua'a*).

According to the story, Kamapua'a one day came to the edge of Halema'uma'u, the giant crater on the slopes of Kīlauea volcano where Pele and her sisters to this day reside. As Kamapua'a stood on the rim of the crater, Pele's sisters looked up and exclaimed:

"Pele, there is a handsome warrior standing up there on the edge of the *pali* [cliff]!"

But when Pele—who most often takes the shape either of a beautiful young woman or a wizened grandmother—looked up, that's not what she saw.

"Warrior!" She laughed. "All I see is a smelly pig!"

Hearing this, Kamapua'a looked down and said something to the effect of:

"Well, all I see is a shriveled old hag!"

And so began a battle. Pele hurled molten lava into the skies and Kamapua'a, who had powers over the weather, summoned the rains in an attempt to drown Pele's fires. In the end, the two fought to a standoff— and came to an agreement: Pele would take one half of

the island, and Kamapua'a the other. Eventually, the two would also take each other as lovers.

So it is that the leeward side of Hawai'i— in general, the area to the west of Mauna Loa and Mauna Kea volcanoes—is for the most part dry, while the windward, eastern side of the island is much wetter. (Hilo, the capital city of the island and the second most populous area in the Hawaiian chain, receives an average of 150 inches of rain per year.)

But nothing about the Big Island, as the largest and youngest of the major Hawaiian islands is known, is so cut and dried. Enclosed within the island's 4,038 square miles is virtually every type of geographic formation, terrain and climate to be found on earth. There are rain forests and deserts here; snow-white beaches and snow-capped mountains. In a day, one can travel from sea-level to above-cloud level, arriving at the summit of Mauna Kea—13,796 feet above the Pacific.

Likewise, each of the island's nine districts has a flavor of its own. South Hilo, on the eastern slopes of Mauna Loa and Mauna Kea, houses the town of Hilo proper, with its low, false-front buildings straight out of a Hollywood Western. (Much of the downtown area has a two-story height restriction.) North Hilo encompasses the southern Hāmākua Coast—a largely agri-

Preceding pages: Hiker enjoys the view of Alakahi Valley from the Kohala Ditch Trail.
Above: The summit of Mauna Kea rises 13,796 feet above downtown Hilo. Background: Palms
of Mauna Kea Beach Hotel's golf course entrance frame Mauna Kea. Opposite top: Ice covered
snow depth-gauge is a reminder that the weather can be fierce atop Mauna Kea.
Opposite bottom: Sunbather relaxes at Hāpuna Beach Park.

cultural area once dominated by hundreds of acres of sugar cane fields, and now home to smaller farming ventures. The district of Hāmākua stretches inland from the northern section of the Hāmākua Coast up to the summit of Mauna Kea and north along the coast, enclosing most of the string of seven majestic valleys that begins with Waipi'o in the south and ends with Pololū in the north. North Kohala, the landmass created by the Kohala volcano (the island's oldest) boasts the tiny rural town of Hāwī (pop. 924), and cool and wet agricultural lands. South Kohala contains the town of Waimea (at one time home to the world's largest privately owned cattle ranch); the seaport of Kawaihae; the famed resorts and pristine beaches of

the island's "Gold Coast" and the long expanses of barren lava fields that stretch to the northern portion of Kona town. North Kona is home to Kailua-Kona, another popular tourist destination. Pu'uhonua 'o Hōnaunau National Park (sometimes referred to as the City of Refuge) and Kealakekua Bay, the site of Captain James Cook's death, are found in South Kona. The district of Ka'ū is best known for Ka Lae (South Point) the southernmost tip of the United States and an area that is home to the lesser known natural wonder of Green Sands Beach. The tiny, former plantation towns of Nā'ālehu and Pāhala are also found here, as is the Ka'ū Desert. The Puna District shares Volcanoes National Park with Ka'ū, as well as encasing the Puna

coastline, which was home to a number of small settlements known collectively as Kalapana before most of the area was inundated by Pele's lava in the mid-1980s.

More than any other island, Hawai'i retains much of the island chain's mythic past. Ancient heiau (temples) can still be found at numerous sites throughout the island, as can petroglyphs—rock carvings that tell the story of Hawai'i's first inhabitants. Ancient rock walls, pieced together by hand without any mortar, can still be seen throughout South Kohala, many to this day being used as property markers for the area's modern settlers.

And there is also a more palpable presence here. In the Keaukaha area, just outside of Hilo town, certain homeowners have learned to leave their front and back doors unlocked. Their homes have been built on paths used by the Night Marchers, legendary spirits who walk the same path over and over, and whose look can kill—and who will bang incessantly on doors that bar their way.

Tales abound of the mischievous works of spirits on the Saddle Road, which connects Hilo to Waimea and the Kona coast by cutting between Mauna Loa and Mauna Kea. Hunters know that carrying pork on this road without leaving a proper offering is an invitation for trouble.

And of course there is Pele, one of the first to arrive in the Hawaiian Islands and one of the longest enduring of the chain's otherworldly inhabitants. It is not enough to say that people believe in the *legend* of Pele. She is here simultaneously as creator—adding many new acres of land to the island over the last decade—and destroyer, burying numerous homes and countless ancient archeological sites in the Puna district since 1983.

This is the paradox and the beauty of the Big Island —a land that has existed for millennia, and yet is still suffering through the process of being born. It is a land that is very much alive.

E komo mai: Welcome to Hawai'i.

Above left: *Kauna'oa Beach, one of Hawai'i's finest.*

Opposite: *Yellow ginger along the ridges above Waipi'o Valley.*

HĀNAU

BIRTH

PELE MAY BE THE VOLCANO GODDESS, but she did not *create* the island she now calls home. The island of Hawai'i existed long before she arrived from the mythic land sometimes referred to as Kahiki Nui. Like all of the 130 Hawaiian islands, islets and atolls (most of which are uninhabited) that stretch across 1,600 miles of the northern Pacific Ocean, the island of Hawai'i is the end result of lava spewing from a single "hot spot" beneath the earth's crust. Over the course of millions of years, this hot spot has remained stationary, while the earth's crust has migrated to the northwest at approximately four inches per year, all the while opening new vents through which lava belched up to create the various islands in the chain—from the eldest (the submerged Emperor Seamount on the extreme northwestern end of the chain) to the youngest (the also submerged Lō'ihi volcano, which is expected to break the surface of the Pacific off the coast of the Big Island in the next few hundred-thousand years).

At 4,038 square miles, the Island of Hawai'i is large enough to house all of the other major Hawaiian islands combined. The island is made up of five large shield volcanoes (so named because their rounded surface is reminiscent of a warrior's upturned shield). The tallest, Mauna Kea ("snow mountain"), rises 13,796 feet above the sea. The others are Mauna Loa ("long mountain"—13,677 feet), Hualālai (8,271 feet), Kohala (5,480 feet) and Kīlauea (4,093 feet). Kīlauea, which has been erupting almost continuously since 1983, and Mauna Loa (which last erupted for 22 days in March of 1984 and sent lava flowing to within four miles of the outskirts of Hilo) are active volcanoes. Mauna Kea and Kohala are considered to be extinct, having last erupted many hundreds of years ago. Hualālai falls between these two categories: Since it last erupted somewhere around the year 1800, it still must be considered dormant—that is, sleeping.

The size of the island and wide range in elevations make for an incredibly diverse climate. Certain areas on the windward (eastern) slopes of Mauna Loa have rainfall that tops 300 inches annually. Meanwhile the leeward coast, dominated by the Kona area, is shielded by the mountains from the rain clouds that are blown in off the ocean by the prevailing northeasterly tradewinds. Some areas of this region are so dry that they are classified as true desert. At the summits of both Mauna Kea and Mauna Loa, snow often falls during the winter months.

Like the youth that it is, the island is still incredibly

Above: Acid rain cloud forms from lava entering the Pacific, Hawai'i Volcanoes National Park.
Background: Lava flows spill into the ocean and make a new black sand beach.
Opposite top: Early morning clouds surround the foothills of Mauna Kea.
Opposite bottom: Mauna Loa and Mauna Kea dusted with snow.

A hiker views the huge steam cloud created by the lava flow to the Pacific. Opposite, clockwise from top left: Hot pahoehoe lava forms unusual patterns on a cliff above the ocean. Older flows dot the prehistoric landscape near Halemaʻumaʻu Crater. Lava closeup shows the unusual color found on this "tree mold." Another tree mold illustrates how fragile and glasslike lava can be.

active. The erupting volcanoes occasionally trigger earthquakes. Most are minor, but not always. On November 29, 1975, much of the island's Puna coast subsided (literally dropping several feet in an instant), triggering an earthquake that topped 7 on the Richter scale.

In the area of the oldest flows, the Kohala Mountains, the lava has long broken down into extremely fertile soil, with the upper reaches of the mountains blanketed in lush rain forest. However, where fresher flows have occurred, geologists and volcanologists have a unique opportunity to literally reenact the creation of the earth. Lava in Hawaiʻi takes on two unique forms—rough and jagged clinker lava (ʻaʻā) and smooth, ropy and wrinkled lava (pāhoehoe). (An interesting note: Because Hawaiʻi

has been so prominent in the advance of volcanology, these two terms have become the universal descriptions worldwide for these types of lava flows).

Today, volcanologists have a chance to further witness the process of island building. Fifteen miles off the southeast coast of the Big Island, Lōʻihi volcano is erupting away. Though still 3,000 feet below the surface, over the past 100,000 to 200,000 years the volcano has risen more than 10,000 feet above the ocean floor, creating a caldera that measures close to three miles across. While it will be many thousands of years before Lōʻihi sees daylight, the volcano continues to bubble in the black depths, reenacting a process that is millions of years old—the birth of an island.

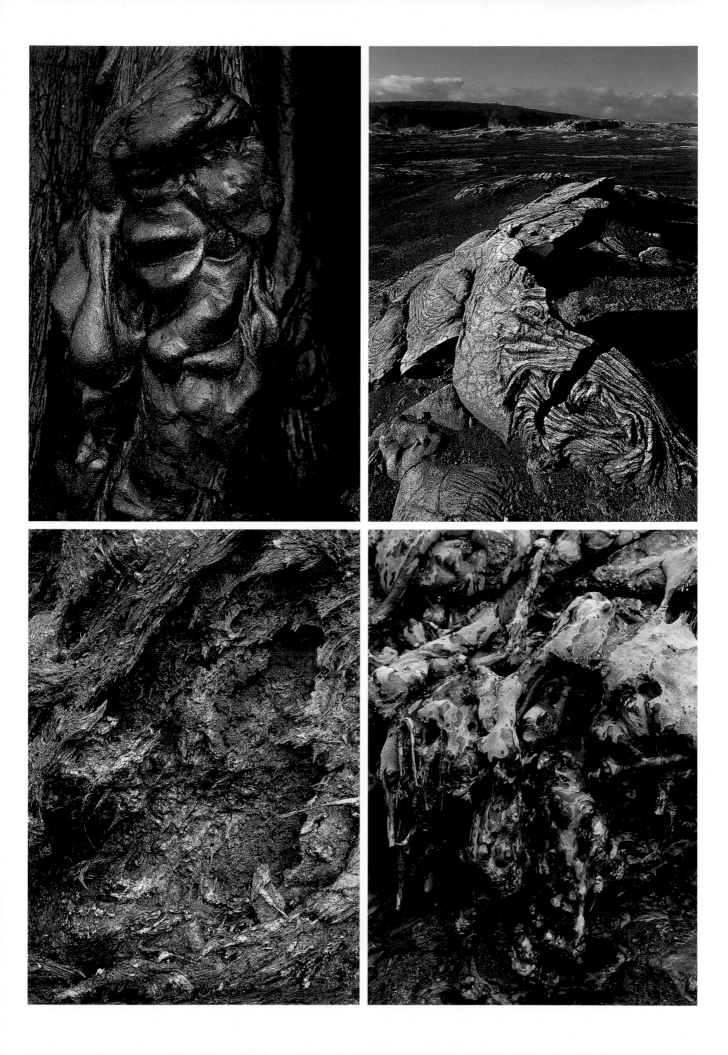

PLACE OF REFUGE

PU'UHONUA 'O HŌNAUNAU

To understand the early Hawaiian *kapu* system, one must first understand something of the larger set of world beliefs of the period. Everything about Hawaiian life was considered to be rigidly regulated by the will of the gods. While the pantheon of lesser gods and goddesses was myriad, there were four major gods—Kane, Kanaloa, Lono and Ku. These gods were considered all-powerful and at the top of a caste system of sorts—followed by a host of demi-gods and goddesses, *ali'i* (high chiefs), *kāhuna* (high priests) and then *maka'āinana* (commoners).

Spiritual power—*mana*—was a major part of the Hawaiian belief system, with the paramount chief holding the greatest *mana* among mortals. The chief's power was considered so sacred, in fact, that commoners could be executed for allowing their shadow to cross the dwelling of a ruler.

Kapu, then, was the system of rules governing behavior among all the classes. While some rules were meant to enforce the hierarchy—commoners were required to prostate themselves whenever a conch shell was blown, signaling the imminent arrival of a high chief—others were of a more pragmatic nature. Some *kapu*, like those that regulated the consumption of certain foods at certain times, were apparently meant to ensure conservation of resources.

The penalty for breaking a *kapu* was not light. Often, the *kapu*-breaker would be sentenced to death —unless he or she was able to reach the safe haven of a *pu'uhonua* (that is, "place of refuge") to be absolved and cleansed by a priest. Pu'uhonua 'o Hōnaunau was such a place of refuge.

Though no records tell when this area 22 miles south of modern-day Kailua-Kona was designated a safe haven, history does note that the great stone wall that encloses Pu'uhonua 'o Hōnaunau was built sometime around the year 1550. Like all rock constructions of ancient Hawai'i, the wall is made of stones that are held together solely by friction—no mortar was used. This is phenomenal when one considers the dimensions of the great wall: 10 feet high, 17 feet wide, and 1,000 feet long. Roughly L-shaped, the northern segment of the wall measures over 600 feet in length, the other leg about 400 feet, with the sea forming the third leg of a triangle. the whole area takes up some 12 acres.

At the seaward end of the north wall was the Hale o Keawe ("House of Keawe"), a temple built about

Above: Hawaiian ki'i akua (deity images) surround Hale o Keawe Heiau,
at Pu'uhonua o Hōnaunau National Historic Park.
Background: A winter sunset silhouettes
the ki'i at the Place of Refuge.

*He-Lei-Palala fishpond
was used to provide fish
for Hawaiian royalty.*

1650 as a mausoleum for the bones of the Big Island's ruling chief—Keaweikekahaliiokamoku. Part of Pu'uhonua 'o Hōnaunau's sacred power comes from the contents of Hale o Keawe—the bones of 22 other chiefs would eventually be placed in this temple.

The safety of all places of refuge was rooted firmly in the Hawaiian system of beliefs. No one, including rival chiefs, dared risk incurring the wrath of the gods by violating the sanctity of a *pu'uhonua*. To do so would mean sure destruction by volcanic eruption, hurricane, illness or other calamity. Once inside the *pu'uhonua*, the refuge seekers were safe from their pursuers, usually the king's warriors. Any pursuer who dared to enter would be in violation of the *kapu*, and therefore immediately slain by the temple priest. Pu'uhonua 'o Hōnaunau served everyone from chief to commoner—not only those who had broken *kapu*, but also defeated warriors escaping battle, women and children, and the ailing.

Right: *These ki'i were carved from 'ōhi'a trees, a wood found throughout the Big Island.*

Pages 18–19: *A fishing boat returns to Hōnaunau Bay, next to the Place of Refuge.*

Above: *Local residents of Hawaiian ancestry recreate a religious ceremony.* Right: *Elementary school kids visit the Great Wall, built sometime in the mid-1500s.* Opposite left: *Hawaiian woman rolls hala fronds together for drying.* Opposite right: *Rolls of hala and tea leaves hang from the roof of a halau, or thatched shed.*

Like the Society Islands, from which the idea of a place of refuge was imported by early immigrants, *pu'uhonua* were considered sacred ground. Their walls were inviolable. Only in Hawai'i, though, could a *kapu*-breaker re-emerge as though nothing had happened and return home to a normal life. Again, this was due to a strong system of beliefs. Just as no one would dare anger the gods by disturbing the sanctity of a *pu'uhonua,* it was also taken for granted that no one would dare to *leave* a *pu'uhonua* without first having made atonement to the gods for their transgressions. The absolution ceremony was performed by the *pu'uhonua* priest, and could take either a few hours or a few days, depending on the *kapu* that was violated. Defeated warriors and army deserters entered the refuge and remained there until the war ended.

Interestingly, safe havens were not limited merely to sacred temple sites. Hawaiian kings were also considered to be *pu'uhonua*—though a *kapu*-breaker who rushed to a king for forgiveness and protection ran a great risk, as the king also held the power of the death sentence. Other royalty could also provide shelter. For example, Queen Ka'ahumanu, King Kamehameha I's favorite wife, was a *pu'uhonua*.

Long before the Great Wall was built, the Kamehameha family ruled the Hōnaunau area, but it wasn't until 1782 that the region began to take on greater historical influence. It was in that year that King Kalaniopu'u, Kamehameha's uncle, died and was brought from Ka'ū in the south to be interred in a spot adjacent to Pu'uhonua 'o Hōnaunau. Later, his bones (and his *mana*) would be added to the others at Hale o Keawe.

Canoe club paddlers practice off
Hōnaunau for long distance races.

Opposite: *This ki'i stands guard*
for Hale o Keawe, seen at left.

Over the next nine years, Kamehameha would wage a bloody war with his cousins Keoua Kuahu'ula and Kiwalo, the latter being Kalaniopu'u's eldest son and heir. Kamehameha overcame Kiwalo and took his lands in 1782 and defeated Keoua in 1791. By 1810, he would conquer the remaining Hawaiian islands, uniting the chain under one chief for the first time and earning his place in history as Kamehameha the Great.

Ironically, the *kapu* system which upheld the belief in *pu'uhonua* would ultimately be dismantled *by* a *pu'uhonua*. In November of 1819, a mere six months after Kamehameha died, his son Liholiho (who ruled as Kamehameha II) dissolved the *kapu* system at the urging of his mother Keopuolani and his step-mother Ka'ahumanu. He did so by a simple act—sitting down to eat with the two women, thereby breaking the *kapu* that forbade men and women from eating together. He then ordered all temples to be destroyed. Only Pu'uhonua 'o Hōnaunau and Hale o Lono (literally "the house of Lono") in north Kona were spared.

In 1920, after more than 100 years of neglect, the Pu'uhonua 'o Hōnaunau was designated a county park and given its popular name of "City of Refuge"—a false identification, it turns out. In 1823, a missionary by the name of William Ellis compared the haven to certain biblical cities of refuge, and the name stuck. In 1978, by order of the United States Congress, Pu'uhonua 'o Hōnaunau was properly renamed, and today it serves as a different kind of refuge—a place where ancient traditions are kept safe and perpetuated, for all to witness and learn from.

MADAM PELE
GODDESS OF THE VOLCANO

Not long after Kīlauea's East Rift Zone burst into eruption on January 3, 1983, the Hawaii Tribune-Herald ran a full color, front page photo, showing the evening sky glowing a furious red. An area one inch in diameter was circled in the upper right-hand corner of the photo, and the headline screamed: "Pele sighted!"

The story went on to tell how an amateur photographer had glimpsed the volcano goddess's profile in the clouds shortly after sunset, and had snapped the photo as proof. Continuing well into the 1990s, the eruption would prove to be the longest

—and most destructive—in Hawai'i's recorded history. Throughout this period, there would be continued reports that Pele was out and about: motorists would talk of seeing an old woman with glowing eyes walking along the volcano highway, trying to hitch a ride. In the Kalapana area, the small coastal community on the southeastern flank of the volcano that would eventually be completely inundated by lava from the ongoing eruption, residents also spoke of an old woman—one who would occasionally come to the door seeking food or drink. The houses of those who were kind to the woman were, for a time, spared by the encroaching lava.

After an especially large eruptive phase, thin, gray-white strands of volcanic glass are occasionally blown into the sky, often settling many miles from the eruption site—these filaments are known as Pele's hair. In areas closer to the actual lava flow, small, highly-polished droplets of lava sometimes harden separately from the regular flow—these are Pele's tears.

The Big Island is the youngest in the Hawaiian chain, and literally the one that is most alive. And while volcanic activity is constantly changing the landscape, adding new real-estate even as it buries ancient archaeological sites, it serves to preserve an important link to the island chain's distant past. The island is alive— Pele walks the land.

The tale of Pele is one of the most enduring in the Hawaiian islands, having survived even when virtually every other deity was cast out with the *kapu* system in 1819. Obviously, this is because her presence is still visible to this day. The story begins with Pele's migration from the land of Polapola (a.k.a. Bora Bora) in Kahiki, through the northwest Hawaiian islands and on down the chain.

Moving from island to island, Pele would dig with her magical 'ō'ō stick (a spear-like digging implement), trying to create a suitable home for herself and her siblings. But her older sister Namakaokaha'i, a sea goddess who was angry with Pele for seducing her lover, followed the volcano goddess—filling her craters with salt water, and washing out Pele's fire.

Above: *Molten lava covers Kamoamoa black sand beach in Volcanoes National Park.*
Background: *Visitors are amazed when lava pours into the Pacific and creates powerful explosions of light and sound.*

It was only at Halemaʻumaʻu, on the slopes of Kīlauea volcano, that Pele was finally able to dig a hole so deep that Namakaokahaʻi could not submerge it—a pit over 1,300 feet deep. It was here that Pele established her permanent home, in one of the world's most active volcanoes, situated within the boundaries of what is today known as the Hawaiʻi Volcanoes National Park.

Here she remains, one of the most powerful figures in natural history and world mythology—and one of the most paradoxical. On the one hand, Pele is recognized as a wrathful goddess, one who is quick to anger and send her destructive lava flowing. On the other hand, it is Pele who protects those who respect her domain—and who continues to give birth to new lands.

Opposite top: *Molten lava from Pu'u 'Ō'ō vent drops into the Pacific.* Bottom left: *'Ōhi'a lehua and ama'u fern.* Above and right: *Pu'uloa petroglyph field in Volcanoes National Park is the largest in Hawai'i, with over 15,000 carvings.*

Clockwise from top left: Fiery red and orange lava explodes along Volcanoes National Park's sea cliffs. Aloha week participants recreate a Native Hawaiian ceremony. Pāhoehoe lava formation near Halemaʻu-maʻu Crater. A hiker follows a Bird Park trail into the ʻōhiʻa forest.

Clockwise from top left:
Conch blowers signal the
Aloha Week festival to begin,
on the edge of Halemaʻumaʻu
Crater. Tourists walk by the
remnants of an ʻōhiʻa forest
on Devastation Trail.
Thurston lava tube. ʻŌhiʻa
lehua bloom along the edge
of Kilauea Caldera.

Pages 30–31: *Steam clouds fill the sky where molten lava enters the sea.* Left: *Hikers stroll across the floor of Kīlauea Iki Crater.* Right: *Steaming Bluffs is active when surface water hits hot rocks just below ground level.* Opposite: *At sunset spectators watch lava explode when it empties into the Pacific Ocean.*

DEATH OF A SEAMAN

THE FINAL VOYAGE OF CAPTAIN COOK

KNOWING HOW MUCH EARLY HAWAIIANS revered their gods, it's not at all surprising that they would think that a man who appeared on what to them was a "floating island," arriving during a festival period devoted to a god whose return to earth had long been prophesied, was in fact a god. This, in the end, was to be Captain James Cook's downfall.

By the time he stumbled upon Kaua'i in 1778, the leader of the expedition that first revealed the existence of the Hawaiian Islands had already made a name for himself in the annals of navigation, through two earlier expeditions. In 1768, Cook had spent six months mapping the coasts of New Zealand and eastern Australia before returning to England via a trip around the world.

On his next voyage, during which he commanded the *Resolution* and *Adventure*, Cook was the first to sail south of the Antarctic Circle—in the process documenting the existence of numerous Pacific islands. After sailing a record three years and covering more than 60,000 miles, the *Resolution* returned to England in July, 1775.

Cook's final voyage was only his third, but with it he became the prime *western* explorer of the Pacific. (Something to keep in mind: While Cook's accomplishments were exemplary in European terms, it's important to remember that the original residents of

the Pacific had already covered most of the same ground hundreds of years earlier, and were far more accomplished seafarers).

For this voyage, Cook commanded the *Resolution*; his consort ship was the *Discovery* under Captain Charles Clerke. After returning briefly to the South Pacific—and noting the existence of Christmas Island—the ships headed northward. On January 18, 1778, the *Resolution* made sight of an island to the northeast, and another to the north. The next day, a third island appeared to the northwest. O'ahu, Kaua'i and Ni'ihau had been "discovered," and Cook christened them the Sandwich Islands after his patron, the Earl of Sandwich.

Trade began with the Hawaiians, aided by the fact that the local language was similar to that spoken by a group of Tahitians who were sailing onboard the *Resolution*. (The similarities in language would later help to confirm the theory that Tahitians were actually the second wave of settlers to arrive in Hawai'i, reaching the islands sometime around the 12th century A.D. and subjugating earlier settlers from the Marquesas islands, who had arrived somewhere between 500 and 800 A.D. Gods and goddesses like Lono and Pele are actually imports from Tahiti.) The Hawaiians were especially interested in acquiring iron nails, which they fashioned into fishhooks.

Unfortunately, there was other trade. Cook tried in

Above: *In Kealakekua Bay a kayaker paddles around rocks on his way to Captain Cook Monument.*
Background: *Low tide exposes lava in the southeast corner of Kealakekua Bay.*

Kids and adults plunge into Alahaka Bay from a lava tube found along the King's Trail in Hōnaunau. Opposite: A local family enjoys a kayak outing in Honomalino Bay.

vain to keep the 66 sailors (more than half of the crew of 112) who had measurable cases of venereal disease onboard his ship and away from the native women. But to no avail—when the *Resolution* returned less than a year later, Cook would note that signs of V.D. were already apparent in some Hawaiian faces.

Captain Cook went ashore for the first time at the vil-

lage of Waimea, Kauai, on January 21, 1778. Here, like everywhere else he would travel in the Hawaiian Islands, he was greeted as if he were one of the highest chiefs. Cook also went ashore a few days later on Niʻihau.

The two ships headed north early in February in search of the mythic Northwest Passage linking the Pacific and Atlantic Oceans through North America.

The mariners spent many months exploring the coasts from Oregon on the American side across to Kamchatka on the Asian side, even venturing beyond the Arctic Circle without finding the fabled Passage. Cook decided to sail south to spend the coming winter in the warm and friendly Sandwich Islands. On November 26, 1778, the ships sighted Maui. Two chiefs who were fighting each other, Kahekili of Maui and Kalaniopu'u of the Big Island, visited the ships separately. After eight weeks of searching for a suitable harbor, Cook sailed on to the Big Island. This is where things began to fall apart for him. (An interesting historical note: While sailing the coast of Maui, one of Cook's lieutenants made detailed maps. The map maker, William Bligh, would himself eventually go down in history as captain of HMS *Bounty*.)

Cook sailed into Kealakekua Bay, some 20 miles south of modern day Kailua-Kona town, on January 16, 1779, at the height of the *makahiki* season—a four-month period of sports and religious festivities dedicated to Lono, the fertility god of the earth. It was a long-standing belief that Lono would one day return to the earth. Cook's arrival seemed to fulfill this prophesy. Effigies of Lono normally took the shape of a small wooden figure perched on a tall mast-like crossbeam with long, white sheets of tapa cloth hung down from the crossbeam. In addition, Kealakekua, considered to be Lono's sacred harbor, was the first spot that Cook chose to land, after circling the entire Big Island in search of a harbor. Therefore, he was treated for a time as a god.

After about a month, however, the visitors had begun to wear out their welcome. During this period one of Cook's crew died, proving to the Hawaiians that the visitors were in fact mortal. William Watman's remains were buried at the Hikiau Heiau, which was dedicated to Lono. (Today, a plaque marks the site, just off the Kealakekua Bay parking lot.)

A series of thefts were perpetrated against Cook's vessels, even as members of his crew were unwittingly breaking various *kapu*. Cook finally set sail on February 4, but was forced back into the harbor with a broken mast barely a week later. When a group of Hawaiians stole a small cutter, Cook made what was to be a fatal error in judgment. Going ashore with nine armed men, he tried to convince King Kalaniopu'u to return to the *Resolution* as ransom for the stolen boat. While Kalaniopu'u debated, another group of marines fired upon a canoe trying to leave the bay, killing a lower-ranking chief named No'okemai.

At this point, the crowd around Cook had reached several thousand. One brave warrior attacked Cook, striking him with a *pāhoa* (a short dagger). Cook drew a pistol that was lightly loaded and shot back, but the charge bounced harmlessly off the warrior's protective straw-mat armor. The marines retreated to their landing boat, but Cook could not escape. (The tale goes that Cook died standing in knee-deep water, the legendary mariner not knowing how to swim.)

Eventually a truce was arranged and the ship's mast and parts of Cook's body were returned to the *Resolution*. (As was the custom, other parts had been distributed to various chiefs involved in the fighting.) He was interred in the waters off of Kealakekua Bay.

Today, a 27-foot tall, white marble obelisk stands as a memorial to Captain James Cook at the northern end of the bay.

BLACK AND WHITE

HILO AND KONA

MUCH OF THE BIG ISLAND is a study in contrasts: Wet versus dry; white sand versus black; "touristy" versus "local." Also apparent are the differences between Hilo and Kona.

It is a bit of an understatement to say Hilo (pop. 37,808) is wet. Averaging some 133 inches of rain per year, it is not uncommon in the winter months for the rainfall from single storms to be measured in *feet*. While schools on the continental United States occasionally have snow days, there have been instances when area schools here have actually been shut down because of the rain!

In part, perhaps, this has helped to preserve the town's sleepy charm. With the downtown area's two-story building limit and a generally laid-back demeanor, Hilo doesn't seem to have changed much in the last 100 or so years. And indeed, buildings like the Haili Church (1859) and the Lyman House (1839) still stand as reminders of a bygone era.

But this is not to say that Hilo isn't without a certain excitement—at least, once a year. Hilo is the home of the Merry Monarch Hula Festival, the celebration of Hawai'i's indigenous dance that is held each year in honor of King David Kalākaua, who was instrumental in the preservation of this art.

In many ways, Hilo serves more as a gateway for tourists than a destination: the town is a starting point for trips to the Hawai'i Volcanoes National Park or up the Hāmākua coast to Waipi'o Valley. Visitors tend to be fewer, and of a hardier variety—a situation which seems to suit the town perfectly.

Roughly 100 miles away, on the other side of the island, Kailua-Kona might almost as well be on the other side of the planet. Everything—the dry climate, the white sand beaches, the hordes of tourists—sets Kailua in contrast to Hilo.

And then there is Kailua's history: It was here that Kamehameha the Great died in 1819; here that his son Liholiho, ruling as Kamehameha II, would break the *kapu*, forever changing the Hawaiian cosmology; here that Christianity was first introduced to Hawaiians in 1820.

Modern Kailua continues as an area of vitality and bustling change. Whereas Hilo, the county seat and second largest city in the Hawaiian Islands, attracts relatively few visitors, Kailua is a major tourist destination. The town has grown up around the visitor industry, and each year plays host to such international draws as the Ironman Triathalon and the International Billfish Tournament.

In the end, there is no black and white. Depending on whom you talk to, Hilo is either quaint or dull; Kona either vital or overrun. Still, each is unique…and each is a living monument to Hawai'i's storied past.

Above: *Tourists stroll along the Ali'i Drive seawall in Kailua-Kona.*
Background: *In Hilo Town a visitor points out the new paint job on the 1910 Koehnen Building.*

This spread, clockwise from top left: *Downtown Hilo and Bayfront County Park. Shoppers hunt for a bargain on Haili Street. Outrigger paddling canoes under repair. The refurbished 1912 Hata Building. A local fishing boat is tied to the pier next to Suisan fish market. Hilo Bay Building.*

Clockwise from top left: King Kalākaua bronze statue. Hulihuli chicken barbecue. Tsunami (May 1960) memorial clock. Wailuku River bridge fisherman. Flower leis for sale at the Hilo farmers' market. Chinese vegetable stand. A fish merchant sells his catch. Fishing boats are moored in the Wailoa River next to Suisan Market. A vendor displays locally grown fresh flowers.

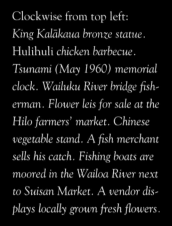

Clockwise from top left: Anthuriums at the farmers' market. King Kamehameha statue with leis. Kīlauea Preserve Center and shop owner. Haili Church (1859) exterior and interior views. Kamehameha Avenue and the Koehnen Building. Suisan fish auction, held every morning except Sundays at 7:30 a.m. Suisan Market dock. Fishermen at the teahouse, Lili'uokalani Gardens.

Clockwise from top left: *Lyman House Memorial and Mission House. A restaurant patron enjoys lunch in downtown Hilo. Boats moored at the mouth of the Wailoa River. Rainbow Falls Park, a popular visitor destination. Opposite: Surf's up at Honoli'i Beach Park. Pages 46–47: The Moku'aikaua Church steeple and Hulihe'e Palace are the most* *prominent buildings seen from Kailua pier. Page 48: The entrance to Hulihe'e Palace State Monument. Page 49, clockwise from top left: Kona Inn Restaurant on a windy day. Moku'aikaua Church (1837). A rowboat tour of Kailua Bay keeps these young men busy. One very pleasant way to tour Kailua-Kona is with this horse-drawn carriage.*

Clockwise from top left: *Kailua Bay shoreline near Hulihe'e Palace. Young fisherman returns home to Honokāhau Harbor. Kailua Bay sunset. Japanese visitors walk along the seawall in Kailua-Kona. Kona Inn shopping complex. Exhausted participants rest at the finish line during the Queen Lili'uokalani Canoe Race. An outrigger canoe races the cruise ship* Independence. *Captain Bean's tour boat enters Kailua Bay.*

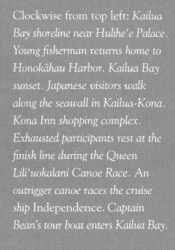

Clockwise from top left:
Kona Inn shops at dusk.
Colorful wind socks for sale
by a vendor on Ali'i Drive.
This sign commemorates
the Ironman Triathlon
official starting point. Kona
Inn Restaurant entrance.
Outrigger sailing canoe heads
for Kailua Pier. Kahalu'u
Beach Park sunset. Helani
Congregational Church (1866).

Clockwise from top left:
Double hull canoe racers.
Young girl enjoys a freshwater
pond at Makalawena. Free diver
swims to the surface. A local
fisherman uses a spear to bring in
an octopus. Makalawena Beach,
North Kona. Opposite, clock-
wise from top left: Along the
rocky Kona Coast a snorkeler
takes a break. Tidal flat and
algae at Kaloko-Honokāhau
National Historic Park. Charter
boat crew brings in a marlin.
Throw-net fisherman waits for
mullet to appear in the surf.
Pleasure boat at Keauhou Bay.
Kids have a chicken fight at
Kūkio Beach. Fishing net,
floats, fins and boogie board.

Scenes from Hōlualoa and Kona coffee country. Opposite, clockwise from top left: *Home with Japanese style architecture. The Kona Hotel. Paul's Place convenience store, downtown. Plant graffiti, Hōlualoa Coffee Mill Workshop. Old post office building, now an art gallery. Coffee Mill Workshop front door. Local farm buildings. Restored butcher shop. Background: Hōlualoa town and Māmalahoa Highway. Above: Flowering Kona coffee trees and plantation. Left top: Picking ripe coffee cherries. Left bottom (left to right): Kona coffee cherry, parchment, green beans and roasted coffee beans.*

HĀMĀKUA

THE HĀMĀKUA COAST, WAIPI'O, WAIMEA

DRIVING THE HĀMĀKUA COASTLINE NORTH from Hilo to Kohala is an experience like few others, offering a window into a rural Hawai'i far removed from the bustle of an urban landscape like Honolulu. Glancing *mauka* (that is, towards the mountains) at any given moment, one can glimpse the ribbon of a rain-fed waterfall dropping into mists of deep valleys; whereas *makai* (seaward), the landscape occasionally gives way to sharp cliffs. In the 40 or so miles between Hilo and Waipi'o (the first of the seven major valleys that carve out the coast between the town of Honoka'a and the north Kohala district), there is a wealth of once-in-a-lifetime scenery—enough to stretch an hour's drive into a day-long trip.

For over 100 years, the Hāmākua coast was the home of King Sugar, the cane companies providing a major source of income for the Big Island economy. Today, sugar is grown much cheaper in other parts of the world, and the cane mills have all closed—the once unbroken sea of green cane stalks now gone fallow, giving way here and there to small islands of diversified agriculture.

Ten miles north of Hilo and a mile or so inland off the Belt Highway, one comes to the town of Honomū and 'Akaka Falls. Once a bustling sugar town that played host to more than one saloon, hotel/bordello and, yes, a church or two, on first glance Honomū has something of a ghost town feel today. Don't be fooled by the false-front buildings that appear to be deserted. A stroll along the (short) main street finds a few very interesting galleries and at least one fine cup of coffee—and even a tattoo parlor.

Just beyond Honomū town lies 'Akaka Falls. The easy, 40-minute walk (the path is paved) is well worth the detour off the coast: On the way to the scenic 420-foot waterfall, pedestrians pass through fragrant stands of ginger, heliconia and orchids, and walk beneath giant ferns and bamboo groves. For the less athletic, 'Akaka Falls State Park is one of the easiest forays into Hawai'i's rain forest interior.

Back on the Belt Highway and traveling north again, motorists come to the first of the tall bridges (100 feet) and Kolekole Beach Park, where a stream fed by 'Akaka Falls meets the ocean, cutting through a small black sand beach. On April 1, 1946, Hilo and much of this area of the Hāmākua coast were inundated by a giant tsunami, sweeping away 159 people and over 1,300 homes. Perhaps the greatest tragedy

Above: The shoreline at Kukuihaele Landing is battered by Pacific surf.
Background: Constant rainfall keeps the coastal area of Laupāhoehoeiki green year round.
Opposite (inset): In a very calm sea a kayaker paddles by Waimanu Valley.

Clockwise from top left: Art gallery and antique glass shop in Honomū. Merchant adjusts her front window display. Restored downtown Honomū (two photographs). Moped driver cruises through Honomū town. Antique shave ice machine entices visitors to come in and try a local treat. Restored downtown Honomū. Opposite top: Akaka Falls State Park trail. Opposite bottom: Windward coast at Kukuihaele.

took place at one of the most scenic areas of this part of the island—Laupāhoehoe Point. A school once stood on this isolated finger of land. When the wave washed in, 20 students and a teacher were swept out to sea. Today, Laupāhoehoe town has been moved further inland and the area once occupied by the school is now part of the State Park system.

Beyond Laupāhoehoe one comes to Honokaʻa, a mini-population center (with a bit over 2,100 residents) that was once a sugar hub and is now best known for its antique galleries and thrift shops. Here the highway has moved away from the coast in order to skirt the seven valleys, and the change in elevation brings with it weather with a distinctly alpine feel to it. The highway actually bypasses Honokaʻa altogether, but this is another town well worth the side-trip.

WAIPI'O

Honoka'a leads to one of the most fabled areas in all the Hawaiian islands, and one of the most beautiful spots on earth—Waipi'o Valley. Over 1,000 feet deep and nearly one mile across at its widest point, Waipi'o has long figured prominently in Hawaiian history. Inhabited for more than 1,000 years, Waipi'o's importance stretches back even further. Wākea, the sky-father who is said to have sired all of the islands, favored this valley. Legend has it that the gods Kane and Kanaloa spent a great deal of time here. The god Lono is said to have come here searching for a bride, whom he found in the form of Kaikilani, a maiden who lived in the shadow of Hi'ilawe Waterfall—at 1,300 feet, the highest free-falling waterway in the Islands, and one of the tallest in the world.

And there are still other legends: Nenewe, a demigod who was part shark and part man, lived near a pool of another waterfall in the valley; Puapualenalena, another demi-god who took the shape of a dog, occasionally made his home here. Also hidden in Waipi'o is Lua o milu, a doorway to the land of the dead. From this doorway, it is said, the Night Marchers enter the world of the living—spirits of the dead returned for an evening to walk the land.

This is the pre-history of Waipi'o, but it also figured prominently in Hawaiian life throughout the centuries. At the time of Cook's arrival in Hawai'i, some 6,000 people lived in the valley, and it is estimated that its fertile soil was producing enough food to feed the entire island's population (estimated to be around 100,000) in times of famine.

A century after Cook's arrival, western diseases had taken their toll on the valley, much as they had affected the native population throughout the Islands.

Page 60, clockwise from top left: 'Akaka Falls. Hāmākua Coast waterfall. Waipi'o Valley Falls. Honoli'i Falls closeup. Page 61: Hāmākua Coast waterfall.

This page, top to bottom: Honoka'a People's Theater. Honoka'a Marketplace giftshop. Honoka'a Landing residential area. Opposite: Waipi'o Valley black sand beach.

Opposite: *Taro farms dot
Waipi'o Valley's interior wetlands.*

Above: *Boogie boarders enjoy the
surf at Waipi'o's black sand beach.*

By that time, only 600 Hawaiians remained in the valley. Today, the valley floor—only accessible by foot or four-wheel drive—is home to perhaps fewer than 100 residents, most of whom are non-Hawaiian. The quiet community exists much as it always has, with terraced fields of taro and other crops flourishing beneath the walls of this mythic and beautiful valley.

Past Waipi'o, the highway turns further inland to skirt the upper edges of the seven valleys, heading into Waimea. Home to Parker Ranch—for years the world's largest privately owned ranch—Waimea is the epitome of mid-altitude ranch lands. It was in this area that the paniolo (Hawaiian cowboy) tradition was born. Even before cowboys were roving the Wild West

of the United States, Mexican–Indian vaqueros (known by the Spanish name "hispaniolas") had been imported from the Mexican territory of California to take care of another troublesome import—in 1793, British sea-captain George Vancouver had introduced cattle to Hawai'i, as a gift to Kamehameha I. By the 1830s, following a 10-year *kapu*, longhorns and sheep were running roughshod over Mauna Kea and in the valleys of Kaua'i. Thus there was a need for a new breed of Polynesian cowboy. Today, Waimea and the North Kohala area are among the last bastions of the true paniolo tradition, and first-rate examples of a slower way of life that has all but vanished from many other parts of the island chain.

Opposite: *Waipi'o Valley
wetland taro farm. Above left:
Hi'ilawe Falls, Waipi'o Valley.
Above right: Wailoa Stream,
Waipi'o Valley. Page 68:
Hikers climb up the Kohala
Ditch Trail overlooking Waipi'o
Valley. Page 69 top: Parker
Ranch pasture surrounds the
foothills of Mauna Kea. Page 69
bottom: Cattle graze on Parker
Ranch near the access road to
the summit of Mauna Kea.*

Scenes from Waimea. Clockwise from top left: Parker Ranch pasture. The Kohala Mountains, a subdivision and a vegetable farm. Harvesting organic lettuce. Opposite left top: Ke Ola Mau Loa Church. Opposite left bottom: Imola Congregational Church (1857). Opposite right: A Parker Ranch rodeo features bull riding and calf roping.

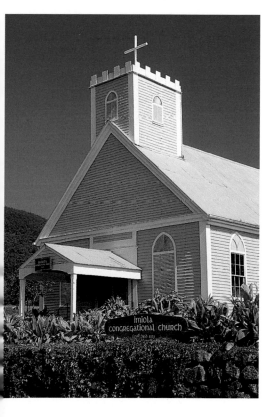

WHILE THE COASTLINE between Kawaihae, on the northern face of the island, and the southwesterly facing Kailua-Kona town is often referred to as the Gold Coast for its string of white sand beaches and exclusive five-star resorts, the archeological worth of this area is greater than a mountain of precious metal. Unlike O'ahu, which has seen many of its archeological sites destroyed by construction, the Big Island is a treasure chest of historical information.

The districts of north and south Kohala are among the richest in historical, archaeological, and legendary materials in the Islands. The area around coastal Māhukona, just north of Kawaihae, has been the site of various University of Hawai'i archaeological investigations regarding Hawaiian life prior to 1800. Further south, in the *ahupua'a* (a traditional form of land division that stretched from the mountains to the sea) of Lapakai, studies have indicated that a coastal fishing village was founded about 1300 A.D. A small group of fishermen lived in houses built on the bare ground and supported by large posts. About 1500 A.D., houses were built on stone platforms with fine pebble floors. At the same time, people moved upland and began growing sweet potatoes and building small C-shaped living areas. Eventually, the uplands were intensively cultivated, and the lowland coastal area became heavily populated. During the 18th century, it is estimated that the area (which today is virtually uninhabited) was supporting a maximum number of people, using all available food resources and possibly pulling together into a district-based political and economic network. Lapakahi State Park today contains the archaeological evidence of these changes.

Around the northern point of the island and into windward Kohala, Pololū Valley marks the beginning of the seven major valleys that extend back to Waipi'o. Standing at the promontory overlooking Pololū's 1,000-foot-high walls, the view southeast is through steep and high sea-cliffs, waterfalls and uninhabited valleys.... That is, uninhabited *today*. Archeological data collected from the area shows that the northern valleys seem to have been initially occupied at the beginning of the 16th century, rapidly attaining a maximum population density and agricultural productivity. It now seems that Kohala Hawaiians may have shifted to the wet valleys generations after farming the leeward slopes and coast.

Kohala was also the first home of Kamehameha I. Though his exact birthplace is unknown, many believe

Above: On a pāhoehoe lava flat in Puakō,
this petroglyph of a man was carved hundreds of years ago.
Background: The fiberglass hulls of outrigger canoes
reflect the setting sun at 'Anaeho'omalu Bay.

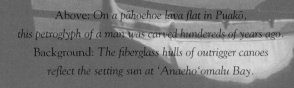

the great king was born near Upolu Point on the
northern tip of the island. The area above Hāpuʻu Bay,
to the southeast, is reputedly home to his family heiau.
The famed Moʻokini (literally "many lineages") heiau
is also found in Kohala, and was eventually rededicated
by Kamehameha. Just to the south, near Kawaihae, are
the imposing heiau Puʻukoholā and Mailekini.

In a very real sense, the Gold Coast was in fact the
birthplace of modern Hawaiian history.

*Opposite top: Puʻukoholā Heiau
National Historic Site is dwarfed
by snow-capped Mauna Kea.
Opposite bottom: Lapakahi
State Historic Site recreates a*
*fishing village of about 1300 A.D.
Above: ʻAnaehoʻomalu petroglyph
field. Above right: Puakō petro-
glyph site, one of the state's largest.
Right: Pololū's black sand beach.*

Clockwise from top left: *Kauna'oa Beach from Mauna Kea Beach Hotel. Waterfalls along the Kohala Ditch Trail. Catching some rays at Hāpuna Beach. Bamboo Restaurant and Gallery sign in Hāwī. Hāpuna Beach lava rocks and swimmer. High surf at Wawaloli Beach. Hualālai Volcano and Hāpuna Beach State Park.*

Clockwise from top left: Self-serve fruit and nut stand. Kids play at the entrance to the Hāwī General Store. Sign over entrance to the restored Takata Building in Hāwī. Pololū Valley and the northeast Kohala Coast. Local sweets on display at a cracked seed shop. The Tong Wo Chinese temple. An art gallery and clothing shop in Hāwī.

GOODBYE, KALAPANA
PELE CREATES, PELE DESTROYS

N O SPOT IN HAWAI'I is a better illustration of what it means to be living on a volcano than the Kalapana area. Falling as it does in the shadow of Kīlauea East Rift Zone, this stretch of coastline along the island's southeast shore—believed to have first been settled in the latter part of the 13th century—actually encompasses the three distinct areas of Kalapana, Kaimū and Kapa'ahu, and has been the primary focus of the volcano's activity since 1955, both in the form of lava flows and earthquakes. Because Kīlauea butts up against the mass of Mauna Loa on its north and west sides, the only way the still growing volcano can move is out and downward, toward the sea. Over the years, the towns along this coastline were subjected to the destructive forces of subsidence (a sudden dropping of the land) and tsunami (tidal waves)—both the result of earthquakes triggered by Kīlauea's activity. Remarkably, for the most part these occurrences resulted in very little loss of life—the notable exception being the tragic drowning of two members of a Boy Scout troop in the early hours of November 29, 1975. That morning an earthquake measuring 7.2 on the Richter scale was triggered by a large subsidence, literally dropping the Scouts' oceanside campsite into the sea—and then overwhelming the campers with a large tsunami.

These deaths were the exception to the norm: Coming over the course of some 35 years, these natural phenomena—while frightening—eventually became part of the fabric of life in Puna.

That is, until 1986.

In 1983, the East Rift Zone began the longest eruptive phase in Hawai'i history. By 1986, lava approached the area of the Royal Gardens Subdivision, to the south of Kalapana proper. By December of that year, the flow had consumed 10 homes and made its way into the ocean—something that many hoped would signal an end to the flow. Unfortunately, another 18 homes would be destroyed between December 17 and 20 of that year. Throughout 1987, 1988 and 1989, intermittent flows would continue to clear homes from the area. In 1987, Punalu'u, a brackish pond more commonly known as the Queen's Bath, would be overrun.

Surprisingly, during this period people continued to buy land and build homes in the Kalapana area, particularly five miles up the road from Royal Gardens, in the subdivision known as Kalapana Gardens. In January 1990, the lava flow took a tragic change of direction to the east, moving away from Royal Gardens and toward the newer subdivision. By March, a vigorous new eruptive phase was pumping an estimated 500,000

Above: Recent lava flow engulfs Chain of Craters Road in Hawai'i Volcanoes National Park, but this road sign survived.
Background: Waha'ula Heiau is surrounded by lava.

cubic meters of fresh lava out of the vent known as Kūpaianaha. At this point, it was only a matter of time before more homes were destroyed. To make a long and sad story short—on April 18, 1990, seven years after the eruption began, the eighty-first structure was destroyed. In the next six weeks, 76 homes would burn to the ground.

This is the way of Pele—simultaneously a creator and a destroyer.

Top to bottom: *Kalapana's new beach is only a few miles from the molten lava flow to the sea. Sunbathers enjoy Kalapana's new black sand beach. The old Kalapana was a favorite beach for locals living nearby. Opposite top to bottom: Waha'ula Heiau survived this eruption, but the visitor center did not. Nothing is left of the Park Services visitor center except twisted steel beams. These abandoned cars are now part of the Big Island.*

YOUNG AT HEART

FROM MAUNA KEA'S snow-capped summit to the black sands of Hilo Bay, from the scorching Ka'ū desert to the lush Waipi'o valley—the Big Island of Hawai'i, like a youngster still in the midst of its first growth spurt, is full of contradictions, conflicting moods, polar opposites and wonder.

That the fire goddess Pele walks the land is a given, destroying monuments that are centuries old even as she creates new lands on which history has yet to be made. To say that a land can simultaneously be at a state of serenity and violent upheaval seems to be an irreconcilable difference, and yet, it is the only way to grasp the nature of this island—700,000 years old, inhabited for at least eight centuries, and yet still a newborn. It's a land of wonder, and one that isn't easily forgotten.

Clockwise from above left: Hula performers, Hilton Waikoloa Village. Hula dancers, Hawai'i Volcanoes National Park. Modern ('auana) hula performer, Tahitian style dancer, male hula performer, all at Waikoloa. Background: Astronomical observatories atop Mauna Kea.
Opposite top: The green sand beach at Mahana Bay is hot, windy and dry.
Opposite bottom: Waipi'o Valley Ridge Trail surrounded by yellow ginger and hāpu'u ferns.
Page 84: Sunset, 'Anaeho'omalu fishponds.